Faith, the Only Star

Faith, the Only Star

✦

A Family's Journey Through Challenge to Victory

Erin L. Hill
Compiled by Rebecca King Craig

iUniverse, Inc.
New York Lincoln Shanghai

Faith, the Only Star
A Family's Journey Through Challenge to Victory

iUniverse, Inc.

For information address:
iUniverse, Inc.
2021 Pine Lake Road, Suite 100
Lincoln, NE 68512
www.iuniverse.com

ISBN: 0-595-29360-3 (pbk)
ISBN: 0-595-65993-4 (cloth)

Printed in the United States of America

To the King Family...

Thank you for your strength, your grace, and your example

Contents

Acknowledgements

Many thanks to the King family for their willingness to share with me their history, both oral and documented. Kathy King and Rebecca King Craig were exceedingly helpful in collecting material and providing a list of contacts—wonderful folks who would help paint a picture of Marie for both me and, I hope, the readers to enjoy. Thanks to Rebecca especially for her desire to honor her grandmother.

Many family members, friends, and acquaintances were generous enough to write letters or speak with me on the phone regarding what Marie had taught them or how she had enriched their lives—thanks to all who took the time to share these thoughts and fond memories. It was my privilege to hear them.

A gracious thank you is due to Visha Ritter, my teacher, my colleague, and my friend, for editing this manuscript.

Finally, I owe an extraordinary debt to my parents, Larry and Barbara Hill, who taught me to love words and a good story, and for encouraging me to write.

Introduction

It seems that I was destined to meet and work with the King family (if I believed in destiny). Unbeknownst to me, our paths were crossing long before I ever began writing their story. My father, Larry Hill, and Jay King most likely played basketball against each other in the late 1950s. My fourth grade math teacher was married to Jay King's high school basketball coach (whose daughter I would later coach and teach). Rebecca King Craig's and my high school volleyball teams played against each other in the early 90s, though we wouldn't formally meet until the fall of 1994, when I was a sophomore and she was a freshman at Taylor University in Upland, Indiana. As a rule, we small-town girls stuck together, and when I learned that Bec (as we would later call her) was from the village of West Liberty, so close to my own hometown of South Charleston, Ohio, I knew we would become fast friends. We laughed to realize that we had competed against each other in high school. Now we really laugh to see where our paths have taken us—back to the small towns to which we said we'd never return. I returned home to teach high school English at my alma mater for six years, and Bec would eventually return close enough (Springfield, Ohio) to work for her parents at their store, Marie's Candies. Rebecca and I remained good friends after graduation, and when she approached me about writing her family's history, I knew the honor would be all mine.

The first time I met Marie King, in the spring of 2002, I was struck by her sense of humor ("I don't want this story to be dry. I want it to be personal and humorous"), her pragmatism ("I don't believe in changing clothes more than once a day"), and her spirit (in a word, spunky). She looked nice for our meeting—wearing floral pants, a long-sleeved knit burgundy top (in a stifling apartment), and three strings of beads in varying lengths that she played with as we talked. Her gray curls were neatly in place (had a permanent two weeks ago), and her bright eyes sparkled behind her glasses. She smiled wide and often. Every so often, she had to ask her granddaughter Rebecca and me to repeat ourselves.

Marie's picture taken for South Union Mennonite Church Directory, 1990.

As I would get to know her over the weeks and the year, I realized that this woman possessed the wisdom of a thousand lives. She knew so much, and yet was so humble. She never took herself too seriously, as would be later evidenced by the stories so many friends and acquaintances would tell. Nephew Merv Zook remembers Marie telling a story, twenty years ago, about falling off a three-wheeled bicycle. "She called it the most embarrassing moment of her entire life," he says, "but the way she could joke about it and take the mishap in such a light spirit made her not only a fantastic storyteller but also a person who could enjoy a good laugh on herself." It would seem so. I would later learn and laugh about times that Marie fell off a pony while riding with her brother Everett (breaking her left arm after already breaking her right arm three weeks earlier), and overturned her bicycle while granddaughter Rebecca was riding with her.

As we began our first interview, I suggested that Marie would probably get sick of all my questions, and of me, before the project was done. She said, "Well, I don't give up on things very easily." So I would learn.

Of course, I expected to learn about Marie as I researched, interviewed, and drafted countless pages—as her biographer, that was my job. I looked forward to getting to know the woman I had heard so much about from her children and granddaughter. My own grandmothers having passed away years before, I even wondered privately if Marie would mind if I coined her my adopted grandma. What I did not expect, however (perhaps naively), was how much I would learn about myself as I went through the biography process. I mean, this book wasn't supposed to be about me, right?

But I found that there were great lessons along the way, which is just another (add it to the list) of the blessings involved in the writing process—surprises that cannot be anticipated. As I worked through interview notes and correspondence from many of Marie's friends, I communicated often with Bec (All of my research was even making sense of Bec for me. I had always admired her intense work ethic and her impeccable personal integrity, and now I understood where it came from). As I worked, I would call Rebecca to tell her about my impressions of Marie or what I was taking away from the story as I wrote. We had a number of meaningful conversations, because we both realized that Marie had so much to offer us as women. We came away encouraged, blessed, and empowered by what Marie had experienced in her rich lifetime. Here was a woman who married, raised a family, started and ran a full-time business, encountered incredible personal challenges, still found time to unfailingly serve others, and *never* complained (a consistent theme in the many letters I received about Marie). Never needed to talk about how "stressed out" she was, never needed to "vent." Never needed to turn to outside crutches to get her through hard times (whether that be as simple as weekly lattes and monthly manicures, or as extreme as codependency and chemical addictions). She simply relied on her family and her faith.

As Bec and I turned these thoughts over in our minds and our conversations, we thought surely she and I weren't the only ones who would benefit from Marie's wisdom. Surely, there is a lesson to be learned for us "modern" emancipated women. I have often wondered if our generation is doing it—"it" being life and all its challenges—better. I don't think we are. Yes, our mothers and our grandmothers made great sacrifices so that we could have the freedoms and the choices that we do today. And I am grateful for those choices. But I don't know that we're doing it better. Sometimes, I think we're softer, a little less-prepared to face life's challenges, a little more prepared to tell others what we're entitled to. Perhaps it's unfair for me to speak for others; I will speak for myself—I know that I am sometimes (often?) guilty of these attitudes.

And so, I have been challenged by Marie—her strength, her grace, and her compassion. Though my life's details are not the same, my response to life can be what hers was—that these days are a gift, that we are equipped to thrive where we are divinely placed, that joy can be found no matter our circumstances. A challenge and a lesson that I hope all readers—young and old, male or female, small-town or big-city—will take away from *Faith, the Only Star.*

"…'ye stars, ye waters…
On my heart your mighty charm renew;
Still, still let me, as I gaze upon you.
Feel my soul becoming vast like you!'…

'Wouldst thou be as these are? Live as they…

Unaffrighted by the silence round them,
Undistracted by the sights they see,
These demand not that the things without them
Yield them love, amusement, sympathy.

And with joy the stars perform their shining…
For self-poised they live, nor pine with noting
All the fever of some differing soul.

Bounded by themselves, and unregardful
In what state God's other works may be,
In their own tasks all their powers pouring,
These attain the mighty life you see…'"

> *Matthew Arnold*
> *"Self Dependence"* [1]

Prologue

The image of a modern-day CEO is often one associated with three-piece suits, sleek office furniture, efficient secretaries, late nights, hard work, and a healthy bottom-line. These images are of powerful men and women who work in big cities and tall buildings. While some wonder about the fate of small business owners left in the wake of mergers and heavy-hitting conglomerates, Jay King doesn't have time to entertain such thoughts. Dressed in his khaki pants and teal Marie's Candies polo shirt, he enters his "office" at 4:50 in the morning, dons an apron, and starts a mix that will soon be slabbed and pulled, tossed and cajoled into becoming the famous Marie's Peppermint Chews. There are orders to place, deliveries to receive, and within a few hours, employees to oversee and customers to serve.

With his twelve-to fourteen-hour days and a work ethic that would rival that of the most intense workaholics, it would seem Jay might be at the helm of one of the world's most powerful companies. Instead, he walks into his small office, once his father's bedroom, which shelves accounts, receipts, and orders from the past ten years. On the walls, wherever there is space, pictures hang that chronicle the growth of three now-adult children; frames have been moved to allow for space for the grandchildren's pictures and drawings. An Ohio State trashcan sits in the corner. Silhouettes of Seth, Shannon, and Rebecca are to the left of Jay's working space, and on a high shelf above his desk, amidst books and memorabilia, files and records, is a plaque that reads "The best thing a father can do for his children is love their mother." The frame directly centered above his desk, nearly eye-level, however, reads from the sixth chapter of Matthew, verse 33: "Seek ye first the Kingdom of God, and all these things shall be added unto you." Though the words are Biblical, I hear them in Marie King's voice.

1

Her Logan County candy shop, Marie's Candies, a monument to small-town life and local businesses, sits at 311 Zanesfield Road/Route 68 as the darling of West Liberty, Ohio, population 1813. A small, local, family-operated business like this one generates considerable interest in the contemporary market—especially a candy business that has been operating since 1956. Nearly fifty years old, the shop represents different things to different people. To some, it is a favorite stop for favorite candies. To others, it is a symbol of all that is small-town life in Middle America. To still others, it is a reminder of strength in times of adversity, of selflessness, of community, of grace in the midst of pain. Regardless, people are never hesitant to ask how the business started, and Marie, Jay's mother, has always been willing to tell the story. So much so that, in her retirement, she has formally spoken about the advent of the business more than one hundred times. Each time she shares with a group, she entitles her speech "How the Candy Shop Got Started or Faith In Spite of Hardship." To her, those two stories are inseparable; she cannot possibly explain one without the other.

Simply told, it is the story of a woman, her family, and their faith.

Family

The only preserving and healing power counteracting any historical, intellectual, or spiritual crisis, no matter of what depth.

—Ruth N. Anshen

Marie's parents, Dan C. and Maude Yoder, on their wedding day,
January 2, 1912.

Marie's baby picture with brother, Richard, and older sister, Geneva.

Marie King comes from a German, Mennonite background in a line of large families. Her mother, Maud, was the third child in the Allgyer family of eight, and Marie, born on June 25, 1916, was the third child of Maud and Dan C. Yoder's six—two girls and four boys. Maud Umble had married Dan C. Yoder on January 2, 1912, in a double wedding with her sister, Barbara—they both married Yoders. And so, marriage took the place of education or traveling for Maud; she had wanted to be a nurse, but many men in the church at that time told Maud's mother that if she went to nurse's training, she would be lost to the Mennonite church. She was not allowed to go, therefore, and she and her sister Eva (Troyer) were the only Allgyer family members who didn't go away to college.

Raising a family became Maud's career. Family life was on the farm (Dan farmed for Marie's grandfather), and all six Yoder children were born at home. As children, Marie and her siblings attended Couchman, a three-room country grade school. She enjoyed the education and accountability she received there; today, she says, "People miss something if they don't go to country school." Even at a young age, she seemed to be appreciative of the small farming community and all it offered. After grade school, she attended Salem Local School in Kingscreek, Ohio, which has since consolidated with West Liberty School to become West Liberty-Salem Local Schools.

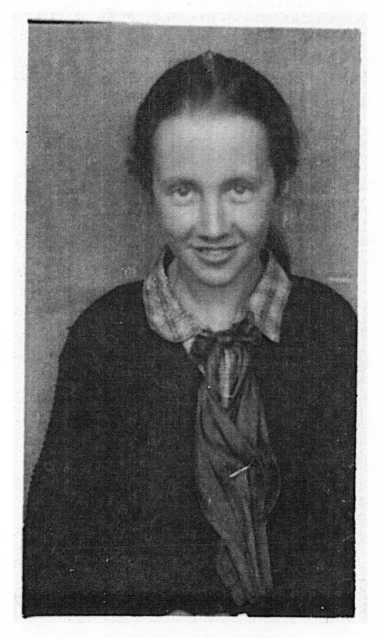

Marie in grade school in the 1920s.

Marie remembers Maud as a caring mother. In 1926, when she was ten, Marie broke her left wrist. Three weeks later, with her arm still in a sling, she fell off the family pony and broke her right arm at the shoulder. Maud fed her for a week until the sling came off Marie's left arm and she could take care of herself. Mama, as Marie called her, even let Marie sleep in her bed while Dan was off helping a neighbor family. During this time and many others with the children, Maud was thankful for the correspondence nursing class she had taken but never finished.

Marie in her early teens on Prince.

Marie also remembers her mother always doing for others (a lifestyle Marie continues today) and fondly recalls making candy with her mother. It was something they enjoyed doing together, and both Maud and Marie loved to give the candy as gifts. At times, they made sixteen different types of fudge to give to friends, family members, and neighbors.

Marie's fudge recipe.

Marie's Penuche recipe.

Marie was close to her siblings and parents, and the family got along well. The brothers and sisters may have had, as she recalls, "a few teases," but they cared for each other and respected their parents. Marie was introduced to hardship early, though; her mother underwent an operation for a goiter and slipped into a coma. All six children went to see Maud in the hospital, and even today, Marie wishes they hadn't. It was difficult to see her mother under those circumstances. Maud never recovered; she died in 1929, when Marie was thirteen, "just when I really needed a mother," she recalls. She admits that she was "jealous that other girls had a mother." While the nation was reeling under the desperation of a stock market crash and uncertain financial times, the Yoder family was dealing with a far more serious tragedy. They had lost a wife and a mother. The youngest child, Danny, was only five at the time.

Though deeply saddened by the loss of his wife and the mother of his children, Dan Sr. demonstrated strength and expected the same from his children. Despite his sadness, Marie says, "He kept us together. He taught us to work hard, honor God, and he loved us—we knew." As he guided and directed his children, he would not permit any pouting or self-pity. He told the children that life was what they made it and what they got out of life would be what they put into it. And so it seemed that Marie was born into a family that was already preparing her for what would lie ahead in the years to come. Without knowing it, Dan modeled grace and strength during a time of grief and difficulty. Marie adds, "Our father expected the best from us, and we tried to give him our best. There was no way I was going to disrespect him. He had it hard, and we used to hear him crying in his bedroom, but never in front of us."

Even though Maud was gone, family time was still important (perhaps more so) for Dan and the children—especially in the midst of a period in history that would later be known as the Great Depression. Discipline was important, and a typical morning saw all six children rising at dawn, doing chores before breakfast, eating, and then having a family time of worship that consisted of Bible reading and prayer. There was also fellowship with the extended family. Marie says, "Our family of aunts, uncles, and cousins, and Grandfather and Grandmother were our support group. We never lacked for love or a listening ear." Their times together included picnics, reunions, ice cream suppers, Fourth of July celebrations, and birthday celebrations that all became fun memories. Marie even remembers several sledding trips on Grandpa's hill that finished with Grandma serving hot chocolate, popcorn, and large molasses or sugar cookies.

Because Geneva, the oldest child in the Yoder family, still had two years of high school to complete when Maud died, Dan felt it necessary to hire help for the housework and the care of the children. He found Bertha Yoder, a nineteen-year-old who was saving money to attend Goshen College in Goshen, Indiana, for her teaching degree. Marie saw this as a blessing and today has fond memories of Bertha. "She was a happy person and loved to do special things for us. She was always happy, always singing. We made candy together and laughed a lot. But she also made us work, and we knew if we disobeyed her, she would tell Pop." Like so many other experiences Marie would have as a young girl and woman, these with Bertha would establish her future in ways she would never guess. She would make chocolates for the first time with Bertha, not knowing that this hobby would later prove to be the lifeblood for her family, and for her son's family.

Marie's icing recipes.

Marie's Cream Taffy recipe.

Several years later, after Geneva married Lloyd Hartzler in 1934, Marie took over the duties at home for both Geneva and Bertha. Her older brother Richard had gone away to college to study medicine (he eventually became a pediatrician), but there were still three boys—and Dan Sr.—at home. Marie cooked, cleaned, washed dishes, canned fruit, vegetables, and meats, and washed, ironed, and mended clothes. Her grandmother was helpful in the midst of all this work; "I would have been sunk…because of all the mending I had to do. Those were the days when I put patch upon patch to make my brothers' pants wear longer," Marie recalls. With her characteristic wit, Marie confesses she did rely on one modern convenience: "We did have a Maytag, and those things were wonderful!" When she reflects, she marvels at what she did then; with years of wisdom and maternal experience behind her now, she realizes that at the time, she "wasn't aware of the responsibility of raising those boys."

Marie and her siblings. From left to right: Jack, Richard, Marie, Geneva, Everett, and Danny.

Still, Marie loved her siblings, and recalls the special relationship she had with each one. Jack teased a lot, especially his brothers, while Geneva was "down to earth, loveable, and always good to us." As adults, Marie and Geneva would maintain their special bond, talking every day. Richard was "a nice guy who would go out of his way to help; he was kind. After he became a doctor, he still helped the family. Everett and I got along well with each other and with Danny. I loved my little brothers…I used to grab them and kiss them. You know boys don't like that, but I think it helped them."

Everett remembers this special treatment. "After our mother died, I always felt a special love that Marie expressed to me. She often kissed me and I remember her taking me to school with her one day. I am sure she has had an influence on my life."

All her siblings fondly recall Marie serving their family. Some remember her learning the valuable skill of "multi-tasking" at a young age. "She liked to read and was known to have a dust cloth in one hand and a book in the other," both Jack and Everett recount. Jack's wife, Ruth, says he would "always remember the good meals that Marie and Geneva prepared, and the mothering that they gave to their younger brothers after their mother died." It seems that Marie also felt compelled to teach her siblings a lesson that she would spend her life conveying to others. As Jack says, "She liked to play church and took the part of being the preacher…A favorite sermon was 'Ye Are the Light of the World.'" Though the parishioners (her brothers) were often found running off during prayer, it was a sermon that would become the theme of Marie's life.

Marie's junior prom picture. She was on the committee to plan
games.

Marie never went to college, never had anyone to push her to go to
college, and didn't necessarily see herself as "college material." School

had always been hard for her, and she had to wisely divide her time between her studies and the responsibilities at home that she took so seriously. If she had gone to college, she would have liked to study education. "I think I would have been a good teacher," she says. In reality, she wouldn't need a degree to earn this title.

While Marie was cooking, cleaning, washing, and cleaning the boys' ears before church, her father would lie awake at night wondering how he would keep the boys out of mischief. He hadn't forgotten about his girl, though; her father was just as concerned when she went out on dates. He wanted to know "where she was going, who she was going with, and what time she would be home." Marie felt those questions were okay—"Perhaps girls today should all have those questions," she says—and she never disobeyed the rules. "I never would have wanted to bring shame to my father." Dan encouraged all his children, and especially his girls; whenever Marie went out, date or not, he would tell her to "be brave." This too would be prophetic advice.

Marie's high school graduation picture.

Winfred's high school graduation picture.

In the mid-1930s, Marie's father began a romance with Belle Stoltz-fus, a lady from Pennsylvania. About this same time, in 1936, Marie, during her senior year, met Winfred King—"a tall, dark, and hand-some man," as she still describes him—on a blind date. Sister Geneva and her husband Lloyd had set them up. When Winfred was late for their date, Marie thought, "Oh, he stood me up!" He had accidentally gone to the wrong house and, as Marie describes, had "almost got eaten up by the dog!" She laughs telling the story, and admits that, when he finally arrived, she was "delightfully surprised by him. He was a sharp dresser, and we always had something to talk about. And, he was differ-ent. He was a gentleman, and he treated me like a lady." Plus, Marie grins to tell, "Winfred always had a little loose cash."

Marie all decked out and ready for a date.

After a courtship of two and a half years, Winfred asked Marie to marry him (offering an engagement watch), and Marie says she "said yes right away." There was a personal shower for Marie, at Ruth Ellen Yoder's house, with gifts of gowns and pajamas. They were married on December 29, between Christmas and New Year's of 1938—just nine months after Dan and Belle were married. A shower was given for Winfred and Marie that was similar to today's receptions with cake and ice cream. A "Belling" occurred a week after they were married. This Mennonite tradition involved waking the newlyweds in the middle of the night and putting them in a back of a truck. Winfred and Marie were driven all over the countryside to the ringing of bells until Marie "caught a terrible cold." The Yoder family was happy for both their father and Marie.

Marie's father, Dan, with second wife, Belle.

Marie and Winfred on their wedding day, December 29, 1938.

Marie seemed to have confidence in Winfred, herself, and their union—no doubt because of their shared faith and confidence in God. "We were a family that would get along regardless…I think some families tear themselves apart."

Faith

Mystery on all sides! And faith the only star in this darkness and uncertainty!

—Henri Amiel

When Marie and Winfred were married, Marie was cooking and managing the cafeteria at Salem Local School. In fact, they didn't have time for a honeymoon because Marie had to be back for school after the first of the year. Winfred worked at the coal yard and feed mill in West Liberty—both of which burned down in July of 1939. Modern families would no doubt describe this as "stressful," but Marie wouldn't necessarily agree. "I don't know. I suppose it was, but I didn't think about it. You just take those things in your stride. In those days, you didn't talk about how much stress you had."

While laborers all over the United States—coal miners, Woolworth clerks, barbers, and GM plant workers—were staging sit-ins for higher wages, Winfred and Marie didn't have that luxury. He and Marie had moved to a farm her great Uncle Dan H. Yoder had purchased near West Liberty, and needed this to be their livelihood. They farmed corn, wheat, and beans; they also raised pigs and chickens so they could have their own milk, meat, and eggs. And while spectators at the 1940 World's Fair in New York City saw cows being milked by machine,[2] it would be years before the Kings would see that kind of modern convenience. Their ten to twelve cows were milked by hand. They couldn't afford to buy a tractor, but they did have a pair of trained, "beautiful horses" to help them do their work. "We didn't have enough money," Marie says. At 86, she joked that was "the story of my life."

Winfred and Marie's first son, Joe, was born on July 17, 1940. While Marie was busy taking care of Joe ("a happy baby with blonde, curly hair"), the house, and the farm work, Winfred was involved at the church as Sunday School Superintendent. With what Marie describes as a "beautiful bass voice," Winfred also sang in a male quartet and the West Liberty Community Chorus. Marie and Winfred would often take picnics together in the afternoons, and Marie remembers a trip to Kentucky for the quartet to record ("the four boys and me!" she laughs). Life seemed to be going smoothly for the young family.

In October of 1941, Winfred became ill. He was cold, and his body ached and itched simultaneously. He went to his physician, Dr. Garver, in Degraff, Ohio, on Saturday night. Winfred had been working behind the walking plow all week, so Dr. Garver told him to rest, relax, and cut back on the farm work; they all assumed the flu-like symptoms would pass with a few days rest.

On Sunday morning, Winfred couldn't get out of bed. Marie was "pretty worried." She put Joe, who was sixteen months old at the time, in bed with Winfred while she went out to milk the cows. Dr. Garver came to the farm on Sunday, Monday, and Tuesday; he didn't seem to know what to do. As Garver and Marie watched Winfred's symptoms progress, it was clear he was getting worse instead of better. On Tuesday afternoon, he called Marie's doctor, Dr. Clyde Startsman, from Bellefontaine, Ohio.

Dr. Startsman came down to run several tests on Winfred. By this time, Winfred was completely paralyzed; Marie recalls him having "great difficulty swallowing" and that "he could only move his head." Startsman diagnosed Winfred with polio, and they called the ambulance immediately—Winfred needed an iron lung (something Marie and he had never heard of before). All the iron lungs in Columbus were taken up, but Dr. Morris B. Martin of Springfield, Ohio, twenty-eight years old and just home from the army, knew how to operate the new iron lung at Community Hospital. At twenty-five miles away, it was the closest hospital with the treatment they needed.

Marie says, "I'll never forget the fast ride to the hospital—the siren was going continuously." She watched Winfred struggle all the way there, while he kept saying, "If I could just breathe…" Though she admits she didn't know much about iron lungs, she did know that it would help Winfred breathe. It seemed they couldn't get to the hospital fast enough to relieve her young husband's pain.

Winfred's mother, Elsie, took care of Joe that night, while Winfred's father, Elba, came to sit with Marie at the hospital once they had admitted Winfred. Marie remembers that night as an anxious one

"Most of that night I spent with Father King in that big waiting room saying to myself, 'God is here with us—this too will pass—is this really happening to me?'

"When Dr. Martin came down to see us, he said, 'There's one chance in a thousand Winfred will pull through.' I remember thinking, 'We will pray. God answers prayer.' And I knew there would be churches praying for us as well."

Once in the iron lung, Winfred's relief was not instant. Letting a machine take over for a normal (and involuntarily, under healthy circumstances) biological process was difficult. Marie watched her husband struggle to let a machine do for him what he couldn't do for himself. "You let it do your breathing…you really have to submit yourself to that iron lung. And that's not easy."

Marie and Winfred, in the coming months, would both learn how an iron lung works. The patient was completely encapsulated in the long, tubular machine, except for the head, which protruded from a tight seal around the neck. "A pump inside the machine caused the pressure within the tube to lower below the pressure of the surrounding atmosphere. This sub-atmospheric pressure then acted upon the chest, causing it to expand; the patient then passively drew fresh air into the lungs through his mouth. During expiration, the pressure equalized to atmospheric, and the patient then passively exhaled. This method of artificial respiration became known as External Negative Pressure Ventilation (ENVP),"[3] and it is what Marie referred to when she spoke of "letting a machine breathe for you."

In addition to Winfred's difficulty breathing, he also suffered from incredible muscular pain—a symptom common in polio sufferers. To treat this pain, doctors and nurses put hot packs on Winfred three times a day. Marie says, "He could not move his toes or his fingers. All he could do was lie there."

Although Winfred was in the contagious ward, Marie was able to see him every day. Dr. Martin assured her that unless Winfred saw Marie every day, he would never make it. He had to have an incentive to live. Marie believed him. "I sure did. I knew he was terribly sick, and he didn't respond very well."

While Winfred was in the hospital, Marie was quarantined for the first two to three weeks. She stayed with Winfred's parents, who were both helpful and supportive during this time of trial. "I never knew anyone who had in-laws as nice as I did. They treated me like I was their own, and I'll never forget that," Marie recalls. Winfred's entire family, siblings included, would be helpful in the months and years to come. Winfred's younger brother Herb was still living at home when Winfred became ill, and he often drove Marie to the hospital to be with Winfred.

While she stayed with the Kings, they discussed the mystery of the illness. No one knew how Winfred had contracted polio. He loved to swim (According to Marie, "If there was a question, 'swimming' was always the answer" for Winfred), and they wondered if perhaps that was how he had contracted the illness. In general, the disease had struck fear in Americans since the turn of the century—partially because of its mysterious contraction, and partially because of its potential to paralyze and kill. It was not a new disease—the oldest clearly identifiable reference to polio is represented in an Egyptian stone engraving over three thousand years old—but is ironically known as a disease of development. The more developed a country becomes, the more likely that country is to be ravaged by the disease. Polio is a microbial infection that is spread by the fecal-oral route (as most microbial infections are). In countries where health and sanitation are poor (especially with sewage systems and water treatment facilities), citizens are generally exposed to microbial infections at a much greater rate, and at a much younger age (usually as children). Because of this early and frequent exposure, the body automatically develops immunity to the bacteria/disease. When a country becomes increasingly more developed, its sanitation efforts are more effective, thus reducing the probability that citizens would be exposed to bacteria such as polio. So, when they are exposed, their bodies don't have the necessary immunity to resist such an infection.[4]

In the 1940s and '50s especially, before the polio vaccine would be developed by Sabin and Salk, the nation attempted to stop the spread of the disease by closing public pools and parks, and citizens in general refrained from using drinking fountains and restrooms. Jay's wife, Kathy, remembers the "Polio Scares" of the early '50s, which were not without foundation—in 1950 alone, there were 33,300 cases of diagnosed polio.[5]

While the polio scare was a national concern, it now became a stark reality for the Kings and the town. During Winfred's diagnosis, treatment, and hospitalization, the community became an integral support system to Marie and her family. Friends from West Liberty who lived in Springfield, Ohio, (whom she hadn't known very well) came and picked up Marie, taking her to and from the hospital whenever she needed to go. Even a sister to one of Winfred's nurses helped provide transportation.

In the hospital, Winfred's care was difficult. Because the iron lung was so new (a lady had just recently donated the lung in her husband's honor), few nurses had been trained regarding exactly *how* to treat a patient through such a device. This was frustrating for many, and if the nurses weren't good, they would quit. Marie covered eight hour shifts when nurses couldn't be there or weren't there. As she looks back on the experience, she describes it as "trial and error—we were all learning."

In all, Winfred spent six weeks in the iron lung, though the doctors and nurses thought it would be longer. After he was ready to be released in mid-November, he had a day nurse who wanted to send him to a treatment center in West Virginia. Marie was pregnant with their second child and unable to make a visit to investigate the facility by herself, so Mabel and Paul (Winfred's oldest sister and brother-in-law) took care of the research. From what they could tell, it looked as if Winfred would be treated well, so they sent him to West Virginia for continued treatment. While he was there, brother Herb made many trips down to visit Winfred. As Herb's wife, Mary Lou King, says, "I guess he drove like lightning…but he was a younger brother and wanted to do all he could. He and Winfred were very close, and Winfred would just pour out to Herb at this time."

In reality, the hospital was not what it seemed to be, and these memories are particularly painful for Marie. "They didn't know how to take care of him—they couldn't even give him a bath. It was pretty desperate. It was so bad that other patients were taking care of him. It was for those who were recuperating, and he wasn't to that point yet. We would never have sent him down if we had known."

In December, Winfred was still in the hospital, and the United States was be shocked by the events at Pearl Harbor that triggered World War II. While young men were fighting for freedom on the other side of the world, Winfred was fighting for his life. Though the circumstances were vastly different, perhaps the emotions—the fear, the uncertainty—were similar. Winfred very well could have identified with a young GI who said, "It's almost over and I'm almost home and I'm scared that maybe a lucky shot will get me. And I don't want to die now, not when it's almost over. I don't want to die now. Do you know what I mean?"[6]

In January, he left the hospital and went to Mabel's house. Winfred and Mabel had always been close, so this seemed a good arrangement. There, he had a day nurse, Emma Kaufman, who still used hot packs on his arms and legs to relieve his muscular pain. Applying these hot packs was a chore, as there was no running water in the house at that time. Meanwhile, life went on with Marie, Joe, and Jay on the way, and the family helped out as they could. Marie's brother Jack came home from the service and farmed for them for a year. He also helped Marie move Winfred—no easy task—before the boys were old enough to help. As Jack's wife, Ruth, tells, "Farming in 1942 was done with horses and little machinery. Jack remembers plowing thirty acres with horses and a *walking* plow. It took him two weeks. The cows were milked by hand." But, in those days, families helped each other, and Marie remembers Jack's kindness. "I don't remember paying anyone for anything. Somebody else must have paid him."

Mabel Hoke, a friend of Marie's, took her to the hospital to deliver the second King son (Mabel's husband, Holly, and Winfred had sung in the chorus together at church). Marie delivered Jay while Winfred lay at home. "I felt sad, but those were the days you never talked about yourself. I didn't tell people how sad I was. I thought that showed a sign of weakness. But people were very good to us. They did a lot of things for us that we couldn't have lived without." Jay, born in February of 1942, didn't smile for the longest time. He seemed so sober, and that worried Marie. "When he finally did smile, we loved it," she says.

Jay spent much of his first two years with John Allgyer (Marie's uncle and former mayor of Plain City, Ohio) and his wife, Mildred. Marie spent so much time tending to Winfred's needs, and John and Mildred, unable to have children of their own, were glad to take care of Jay. In fact, they even considered adopting him at one point.

In April, Winfred was moved from his sister's house to his home with Marie and the boys at the farm. Marie learned to help the nurse take care of him. Because Winfred was such a large man, it took both the nurse and Marie to handle him. They moved him from side to side while in bed or to get him into his wheelchair. Physically, it was challenging for Marie to lift Winfred. The community, ever attentive to the Kings' needs, knew that Marie needed help. An older man in town, Uriel Yoder, made a mechanical lift for getting Winfred in his wheelchair and back in bed again that helped eliminate the stress and number of times Marie lifted him a day. She was grateful for this help.

By that October, the Kings had moved into town and sold all of their farm animals, including Nelly and Dutch, the horses, the colt, and the farming equipment. They would live in town for roughly eight years, as Winfred learned to adjust to life under new circumstances. A bright spot in the midst of such trying times was the birth of Daniel, their third son, in 1945.

Marie's faith was integral to her during the time of Winfred's illness and hospital stay, and during this time when family life began looking so much different than she had ever imagined it. Marie says, "So now we had a system worked out that I could handle Winfred myself, and God would give me the strength.

"Winfred never complained to other people. He hated his situation. He hated that he had to be waited on. He hated that I had to feed him. He hated all that—I knew it. But he didn't say so all the time…if he complained, it was to me, because I had to do so much for him."

During the mid 1940s, after all of Winfred's hospital stays, they realized that he would never walk again. Winfred seemed depressed as he came to understand that a hospital bed, a wheelchair, and bedpans were going to be a part of his life forever. "During this time, Winfred didn't smile much, and it was one of the darkest times of my life. I didn't dare think of tomorrow; I only lived one day at a time. It was hard to laugh and have fun with my children, because I knew unless God performed a miracle, Winfred was always going to be an invalid. This was going to be *forever*.

"It would have been so easy to give up. But one thing was important—Winfred understood me better than I understood myself. He knew I had to reach out to others, to give of myself to someone else outside of my own little family. So he insisted that one day a week, I would reach out to someone sick or elderly—a cake or pie baked, cookies or candy given to someone to cheer them up. This really helped; it took my mind off my circumstances."

Friends Shirley and Sanford Yoder saw Marie live out this desire to help others. "Besides the roles of mother, wife, homemaker, and nurse, she also…had a great interest in her church and community. Often she was taking someone to a doctor's appointment, preparing a casserole for someone, or just visiting. We knew her life was very difficult, but you never heard her complain. She had to have discouraging times, but we didn't see it."

◆   ◆   ◆

In 1947, the Bureau of Labor Statistics reported that nearly half of the adult female population of the United States was idle;[7] Marie King was not in that group. She didn't have time to be idle. Marlon Brando, Billy Graham, and Jackie Robinson would all start their American legacies about this time; so would Marie King. In the spring of 1950, Winfred, Marie, and the family moved to a small home in the country, a mile and a half from town, with five acres of land and a large barn. Both Marie's and Winfred's fathers thought this would be a good move for the family, especially for the three boys, who were five, seven, and nine years old by this time. "Without the support and help from our fathers and our families, we could never have done this," Marie claims. It also was a good move for Winfred, as he loved the country.

A common sight was Winfred in his wheelchair, being pushed all over their five acres by Marie or one or two of the boys. Through all of these challenges—Winfred's illness and treatment, several moves, learning to take care of a disabled father—the children seemed to adapt and adjust. Marie says, "It's amazing what children accept…They're better at it than adults sometimes."

Marie with sons, Dan, Jay, and Joe. Winfred's wheelchair is in the trunk of the car.

Jay doesn't ever remember any ridicule from schoolmates about his father's illness. In King fashion, he seems to only remember the positive. As young boys, he, Joe, and Danny would sit on the end of Winfred's bed, and their father would sing to them. Winfred encouraged Marie to take the boys swimming, and they often went to Lakewood Beach, near Springfield, Ohio, stopping for a bag of Crabill's hamburgers on the way back. Family "vacations" also included summer trips to visit family friends Stanley and Helen Yoder in Scottdale, Pennsylvania, and Sanford and Shirley Yoder in Middlebury, Indiana. The boys loved the trips, and Marie says, "The change of scenery was good for Winfred."

There were also family traditions of dinners together every night, Marie's homemade cakes for birthdays, August Allgyer family reunions, visiting cousins, and sledding in the winter. Long before the candy business officially started, Danny recalls Marie making cakes for Milner's Cafeteria in Urbana, Ohio. "I remember, as a small boy, riding in the middle of the back seat of our car, completely surrounded by cakes."

As much as Winfred encouraged the family's fun, he also encouraged the boys to work. Jay recalls, "He couldn't stand to see idle boys when Mom was so busy all the time." Joe, Jay, and Danny, from a young age, spent lots of time "scrubbing floors, cleaning house, and washing dishes—because Mom had so much to do." He also protected and nurtured Marie. "Dad would try to make sure that Mom could take a nap or read, have some time to herself on Sunday afternoon; we were supposed to leave her alone then. I also remember that Dad would never let us sass Mom or backtalk her." Marie could hold her own, though. She didn't hesitate to discipline the boys, and Jay remembers, "She was strong. In a game of Mercy, she could take us down to the floor.

"Sometimes I was embarrassed that my dad was in a wheelchair, but I never felt like we were poor, impoverished, or different from other families because my mom did the work. She still allowed Dad to be the head of the house. We always said Dad was the brain and Mom was the brawn. Dad wouldn't let us forget how important Mom was."

Dan, Jay, and Joe ready for Sunday School.

According to Marie, life out in the country again "gave Winfred something to live for." There were always repairs to do, fences to build, yards to clear, or brush and partly dead trees to cut down. "But Winfred often said it was so much harder to tell the boys or me how to do things—he just wished he could do them himself. It was so frustrating for him."

Kindnesses and help from the community would become a constant. Marie tells many stories of the people who were so good to her family. "I will never forget the first Christmas we lived on the farm. That morning we noticed one of our close neighbors, Floyd Umble, leading a red cow with white spots up the road. This man and his wife and sister had decided that, with three hungry boys around, we needed a cow. That's how we got Rosie—and she provided all the milk, cream, and butter we needed." With a broad smile and a wink, Marie remembers, "The boys' hands were too small to get any milk out of Rosie, so guess who got that job?"

Additional help on the farm came from a former classmate of Winfred's who lived across the fields and had a large herd of Holstein cows. He invited Marie to come over whenever she needed cow feed, and she did. If she didn't come over for feed when he thought she should, he would tell her about it.

One Christmas two of the boys were sick, so the family couldn't go away or have company. Marie didn't feel like putting up a tree, but neighbors arrived with a tree on Christmas Eve—apologizing that it was the only one left in town and had one flat side. This didn't matter to the Kings; Marie says, "We thought it was beautiful."

The family had no professional means of support at this time, but they did have these friends, family members, neighbors, and fellow church members. Brother Everett was moved by Marie's example throughout this time. "She had a great faith in God, facing her husband's illness and her responsibility to her three sons…And people were good to Marie and her family."

Businesses in West Liberty were just as supportive as family, friends, and neighbors. The Kings were often given discounts on products and services they needed. Marie is particularly thankful that the electrician always made sure they were "well-lit." In fact, she claims, "I must admit only through God's grace could I be brave enough to go out to the barn at night to check on the sheep, cows, and chickens by myself. When I got married, I was afraid of my own shadow…but now with a family, I didn't dare show my fear!"

The country home and first candy kitchen and shop, south of West Liberty, Ohio.

Marie could not go out and get a job—taking care of Winfred and the three children was a full-time job in itself. To make money, they tried raising chickens, making use of their five acres and three-story barn located on Route 507. Friends Kent and Dotty Atha did what they could to help. Pat, Kent and Dotty's daughter, recalls that her father "helped with the chickens, sorting out the ones that were aggressively involved in the 'pecking order,' something none of us can imagine Daddy helping with!" Later, the Kings tried raising hens. They also poured cement, trimmed trees, and rolled lawns; however, none of these proved to be significantly profitable, though Marie and the boys worked hard. During these lean years, family, friends, and neighbors continued to provide for the Kings. Gifts of money, food, and clothes were common, and Marie admits she had to swallow her pride. "It was not easy to accept everything for my family. It was a very humbling experience to always be on the receiving end, but we realized we were in God's hands and we were to be thankful. Winfred and I never gave up praying for his healing; though God did not answer our prayers that way, He was taking care of us."

Pat Atha Williams says Marie is "always full of joy, and has been since we first remember her. We also remember being surprised at this because caring for an invalid husband…and three growing, energetic boys couldn't have been easy."

Marie and Winfred with their bow-tied boys, Dan, Jay, and Joe.

Winfred, in an interview with Pastor Roy Koch, said that accepting help from people was something they did humbly. "We realized it was God's way of taking care of us. I don't remember that we ever had to ask people for anything. They were observant and gave us what we really needed. It is almost unbelievable; it is a miracle in itself how God helped us. His hand has been evident in it all."[8]

Marie claims that she and Winfred took comfort in specific promises through the uncertain times. "Three verses in Philippians stand out as having meant so much to us during this time period: 'Be careful for nothing, but in everything, by prayer and supplication, with thanksgiving, let your requests be made known to God'; 'I can do all things through Christ which strengthens me'; and 'But my God shall supply all your needs according to His riches in glory by Christ Jesus.' So we claimed God's promises. We found God was always on time. He never let us down. We found people might disappoint us, but God was true to His promises."

Those promises, and "our deep faith and our love for each other," she says, were the only reasons she and Winfred were able to come through such hard times.

Winfred, five years before his death, shared his thoughts about Marie with Koch. "She was very good at cheering me up even in my darkest hours. She can do that better than anyone else I know. I don't appreciate her enough; I know I don't. She is the one who raised the family. I didn't. No one can do anywhere near what she has done. She would be ahead without me; I was only a burden, but she never let me feel that way."

◆   ◆   ◆

Friends, neighbors, and community members continued to be good to the Kings. Shortly after Dan was born, Marie and Winfred wanted to find a way to thank people for all they had done. "Since I had always made candy, we decided to make it and give it to our many friends, neighbors, relatives, and business people as thank-you gifts at Christmas for the many wonderful ways they had helped us. I made and gave away over fifty pounds of candy every Christmas for almost ten years."

In February 1956, Marie was at the meat locker in West Liberty. During casual conversation, an acquaintance, Floyd Yoder, told Marie that a man named Charlie Nelson had been making candy, but had changed jobs and wanted to sell a chocolate dipping table, a Peppermint Chew cutter, and some chocolate and glucose for making candy. He said, "Why don't you go into the candy business, Marie?"

Marie came home and told Winfred about it. He was skeptical. Winfred said, "[Candy] is a luxury item, and Mennonites are pretty frugal."

Still, Marie and Winfred thought they should pray about it. They talked to their minister, Stanley Shank, and he agreed that prayer was the best course of action. He also agreed, though, that candy was a luxury item. "So we prayed about it," Marie says. They also consulted a few special friends, and stayed up late talking about the potential of this as a financial support for the family. "We needed to earn a living, but who would have thought that candy-making would have been the business I would have gone into?"

After much prayer and thought, Marie spent one hundred borrowed dollars for Charlie Nelson's equipment. He taught her how to make Peppermint Chews, and she recalls the first year particularly being a "learning process." She did not view it as a high-risk investment at the time, reminding herself that this wasn't a lifetime commitment.

The "business," which Winfred insisted would be called "Marie's Home Made Candies," started with nut clusters and Peppermint Chews, pulled mint and molasses-flavored chewy candy dipped in milk chocolate, dark chocolate, or white candy coating. These candies had been made famous by Mr. Dick Kerr (1879–1951), who sold them at Kerr's Candy Kitchen—a favorite after-school hangout for students in the '30s and '40s—in the neighboring Urbana, Ohio. Movie stars who put on Vaudeville acts in Urbana would leave and, upon returning home, would promptly send for more Peppermint Chews. Nelson had worked for Mr. Kerr and gave Marie the recipe. Marie says, "At the time, I thought, 'Surely this was a gift from God—I know of no other candy shop that makes these.'"

Though Marie had grown up making candy with her mother and Bertha, the learning curve was still great. Marie taught herself how to dip candy with her fingers instead of using a fork and a double boiler. The Kings' kitchen was where the candy making took place, and a small room off the kitchen served as the "candy shop." Anyone coming for candy came through the kitchen, so Marie was conscious about leaving messes. When the boys were small, friends and neighbors would sometimes take the boys while Marie worked. As they got older, though, Joe, Jay, and Dan helped wash pots, pans, and dishes, and pulled Peppermint Chews before going to school in the morning (not without a few powdered sugar fights along the way). Jay recalls the kindness of the neighbors—they made a small stool for the young boys to stand on so they could reach the sink and wash dishes. When the boys returned from school in the afternoon, they would pack Peppermint Chews in boxes—an activity that, on more than one occasion, became a race to see who could pack the most boxes the fastest. Before going anywhere in the evening or retiring for bed, they would chop the chocolate to be melted for the next day's candy. Meanwhile, the farm continued to be an ideal place for the King family—the boys worked with their FFA projects, raised Angus cattle, and worked for local farmers in the summer. They even made their own basketball court (with Winfred sitting by, giving instructions), and put a picket fence up to keep Danny in the yard.

Marie and Winfred making Nut Covered Creams. Jay, Dan, and
Mabel King in the background.

"You worked every day just as hard and fast as you could, and it was tiring, because when we started, I was doing most everything myself," Marie says. Cooking, forming, dipping, packing—Marie was doing it all. The boys started helping in the evenings once they were old enough. Marie knew that making the business work would require sacrifice and long hours: "Nobody ever said it was going to be easy."

Once Marie started making candy officially, people started coming to the door to get it, right to the kitchen. "I didn't like when people would come to the door while we were eating dinner," recalls Jay. He knew, though, that this endeavor was turning into a business when they would "come home from school and see the front porch stacked with bundles of boxes. That meant it was time to change your clothes, take boxes to attic, and do chores…I don't know that I thought that it would ever be a family business, but I felt good about it, that this was how we were supporting ourselves."

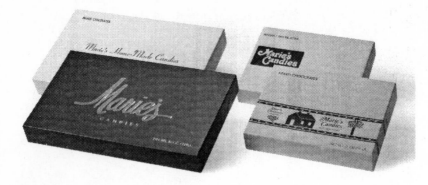

Progression of Marie's Candies box logo from beginning to present.

John and Tom Detwiler also remember the King family during this time, as they lived across the road from them as all the boys were growing up. Joe, Jay, Danny, Tom, and John would play together and ride to school together, and the Detwilers and the Kings would spend some time together as families. Tom recalls that Joe and Jay always brought along a sack of uncoated Peppermint Chews for the ride to school, "and we liked them just as well without the chocolate." There were barbeques and baseball games, and both John and Tom today say they feel privileged to have had Marie as a neighbor, and still today, as a friend. "Our lives have been enriched by our having known her," says Tom.

For the boys, growing up was filled with simple pleasures. As an adult, Danny would say to Marie, "You know, we were poor, but we didn't know it," while Marie recalls, "At that time, our wants weren't as great as they are now." The boys received hand-me-down bicycles from neighbors, but they never complained about not getting something or being poor. From both Marie and Winfred's example, they learned how to be thankful for what they had.

Marie and Marjorie Roby hand-dipping toffee. Margaret King in the background.

In the fall of 1956, business was good enough to build an entrance in the side porch and make the candy room a little larger. Family continued to be a support; Winfred's two sisters, Margaret and Mabel, worked for the shop at this time. (His sister Freda, who married Carl Slonecker, also helped by taking care of the family's ironing.) During the Easter season in 1956, they made and sold more than one hundred cream-filled eggs. During the first Christmas, they made and sold over twelve hundred pounds of boxed candy, all made by hand. Each consecutive year, Marie tells, "We would make all we could make, and we would run out of candy."

Marie's Home-Made Candies
WEST LIBERTY, OHIO
We Specialize in Quality Home-Made Candies

CLOSED SUNDAYS

KIND	COATING	PRICE
PEPPERMINT CHEWS	L. D. R.	$1.90
TURKIN'S	L. D. R.	2.00
CHOCOLATE DROPS	L.	1.75
NUT COVERED CREAMS	L.	1.95
GINGER	L.	1.95
OPERA CREAMS	L.	1.75
BUTTER CREAMS	L. D.	1.75
MAPLE CREAMS	L.	1.75
ASSORTED CREAMS	L. R.	1.80
PEANUT CLUSTER CREAMS	L. D.	1.80
COCOANUT BON BONS	R.	1.80
NOUGAT	L.	1.80
CHERRIES	L. D.	1.90
PEANUT BUTTER FANCIES	L. D.	1.80
PEPPERMINT PATTIES	L. D. R.	1.75
TING - A - LINGS	L. M.	1.75
CHIPS	L. D. R.	1.75
CINNAMON STICKS	L. R.	1.75
TOFFEE	L.	1.90
ORANGE PEEL	L.	1.80
PECAN CLUSTERS	L. D. R.	2.10
CASHEW CLUSTERS	L.	1.95
PEANUT CLUSTERS	L.	1.50
MIXED CLUSTERS	L.	1.95
CARAMELS	L.	1.75
RAISIN CLUSTERS	L. R.	1.50
COATED MARSHMALLOWS	L. D.	1.50
ROCK CANDY	8 Flavors - Colors	1.40
BLACK WALNUT FUDGE		1.60
MINTS - Round in Assorted Flavors & Colors		1.35
ASSORTMENTS	L., D., L. & D., R., R. & L.	
1 Lb.		1.90
2 Lbs.		3.70
ASSORTMENTS 3 Lbs.	L. & R., L. & D.	5.50
ASSORTMENTS 5 Lbs.	L. & R., L. & D.	9.00

Special boxes for special occasions such as Valentine, Easter, Mother's Day, etc. We charge for wrapping and mailing plus postage. Not responsible for goods damaged in the mail.

Please enclose addressed mailing labels with any order to be sent and signed enclosure cards if desired.

L. – Light   D. – Dark   R. – Rainbow   M. – Mint

Early price list.

Even during the chaotic start of a "new business," Marie still found time to do for others. It seems that she could never forget all that others had done for her. Merv Zook recalls a King Christmas dinner in 1957. They all sat around "their big dining room table loaded with gobs of food. As a newcomer to the family tradition, I couldn't help but sense the spirit of hospitality and camaraderie present that day and the 'take charge' spirit of Marie as she orchestrated the serving as well as met Winfred's needs."

◆　　　◆　　　◆

It didn't take long for Marie to realize that she would not be able to run the business by herself. In addition to Margaret and Mabel's help, she hired Marjorie Roby from Degraff, Ohio, the wife of a good friend of Winfred's in high school. Her children were in college, and she welcomed something extra to do, so Marie taught her how to dip. Of the three women, Margaret was the bulwark, though—she would continue to work for the business into the seventies, even after Jay took over. The Kings describe Margaret as consistent, steady, and efficient. "She was so faithful, and never wanted to take off any days, not even holidays. Margaret wanted to work all the time—she wanted to work all the time!" Marie says.

Marie was thankful for the help the women provided. "We were fortunate to have such nice people working for us. When the Lord blesses, you have to pass it on. You couldn't take advantage of people."

The business continued to grow, and with a husband and a family to take care of, it would seem probable that Marie felt overwhelmed. She, however, defers. "No. No, I don't ever remember feeling that way. You just sort of took it as it came." It also helped that, by this point, Marie wasn't afraid to ask for help if she *was* feeling overwhelmed. "I was never too proud to ask. All those years, you just buried your pride and did what you had to do."

Marie tells the story of the Three C's deliveryman who brought their chocolate. She had to talk him into bringing chocolate onto the back porch (it wasn't good for the chocolate to sit out in the weather), because the boys weren't old enough to lift the heavy boxes or were at school when they arrived. The deliveryman seemed reluctant and asked, "Isn't there anyone around who could do it for you?"

As Marie still says today, it always pays to be nice. Marie gave the deliveryman a bag of candy, and the next time he came, he said, "Now ma'am, where do you want this chocolate?" Today, the Kings still share their candy with everyone who helps them—from employees to deliverymen. Marie says, "People appreciate that. They know you appreciate what they're doing."

Marie knew that the candy making was going well, but she tried not to look too far ahead. "You worked as hard as you could work, did the best you could do, and took one day at a time." However, the business did continue to grow, and Marie and Winfred were confident that God was blessing them, even though they were selling a "luxury item." Two years later, in 1958, they enlarged the candy shop to a twenty by twenty room. Everything was done in this room except for cooking and roasting the nuts, which still took place in the kitchen. By this time, the Kings had eight employees.

They kept long hours, and the shop was open Monday through Saturday, 8:00 AM to 9:00 PM. Many customers traveled long distances, often arriving in the late afternoon or early evening. The country drive was appealing for city customers. In addition to their long hours, word-of-mouth advertising and free samples also served the shop well.

Margaret King pulling Peppermint Chews.

Eventually, Joe, Jay, and Dan all left for their own full-time jobs or college, and the business continued to grow. Marie did not have any expectations for the boys regarding the business. "You can't keep children at home. They have to have a life of their own." Margaret absorbed most of the boys' jobs, and began pulling Peppermint Chews every morning (a job she was reluctant to give up later in 1973 when Jay returned). The house itself was filled with the activity, smell, and supplies of candy making. The attic served as storage for empty candy boxes, and an air-conditioned room on the second floor housed the boxed candy. After ten years of business, things were still growing—everything but the house, that is. "Everything was so crowded!" Marie recalls. "We knew some changes had to be made."

Their farmhouse was aging and constantly needed repairs; with the business and Winfred, it was just too much upkeep for Marie. By 1966, the boys were grown and gone, and both Marie and Winfred thought being in town would be better for business.

Carpenter Bill Hostetler drew up some plans for building a new candy shop and home in town if they could find the right spot. After much prayer, they found the right spot. The plans were all made according to the Kings' needs. Everything had to be measured before building began to make sure all the candy equipment and Winfred's wheelchair would fit. The convenience of the candy shop adjoining their home allowed Winfred to come out and help plan and oversee the work. According to Marie, "The wisdom in planning this new shop had to have come from God! In Proverbs, we read, 'For the Lord grants wisdom…His every word is a treasure of knowledge and understanding…He grants good sense to the godly…His saints…He is their shield, protecting and guarding their pathway…He shows how to distinguish right from wrong…God blesses those who obey Him…Happy is the man who puts his trust in the Lord."

In May of that year, 1966, Winfred suffered a nervous breakdown and was hospitalized for two weeks. Marie attributes this to all his worry about the business and their decision to build. "Something snapped in his mind," Marie says. "He worried and couldn't sleep at night. I would sit in the stairway during the day as I called the doctor so Winfred wouldn't hear. In the hospital, they didn't know how to take care of such a helpless man. It was a terribly scary time.

"During his hospitalization, I had to make up our minds about our readiness to build. Since this involved borrowing a large sum of money, we could not make a snap decision. But everyone close to us knew that since the business had grown so much, we could not stay where we were. So I said, 'Yes, we will build!' God had been so real to me in all of this, I had faith to believe it was the right thing to do."

Jay worked with the carpenter on the new building, while townspeople came every night to check the progress of the building. Marie recalls the financial strain of building, and though the business had helped provide a means of income for the family, she says, "We still weren't making enough money, and I can't say enough about the community during this time. We couldn't have survived otherwise, because thinking you're tough and being tough are two different things!"

As they had done so many times before, the community would see a need and tend to it—before Marie and Winfred needed to ask. Marjorie Roby collected contributions from townspeople to purchase an electric hospital bed for the Kings. Marie admits that it was so much easier to care for Winfred with that convenience. Winfred's sister Mabel also continued to be a support to Marie. "I needed her. She was a real asset to me. I don't know what I would have done without her." Mabel's husband, Paul, always helped with odd jobs before he took her home.

Workers began digging the foundation for the new home and shop on July Fourth, 1966. There was no turning back then. "I said go right ahead. By that time, I had hashed it over and worried about it so much." And when Winfred knew that the work had begun, Marie recalls, "He was like a new person." He could finally quit worrying. The new shop and home were ready by that Christmas, and Winfred and Marie moved in before New Year's Day. "Truly, we could hardly believe how everything fit just like we had planned. We thanked and praised the Lord. God really had given us wisdom."

New facilities—home and candy shop in town, at the north edge of
West Liberty, Ohio, on Route 68.

Not only had Winfred worried about building—he was also concerned about his wife. He knew that, practically speaking, the execu-
tion of the business all depended on Marie. She rose between five
o'clock and five-thirty every morning, cooked all the candy necessary
for the day, came in to prepare Winfred's breakfast, bathed, shaved,
and dressed him, and made him comfortable for the morning. He took
calls for a local farmer who was in the artificial insemination business,
as well as calls for the candy shop. He also kept the books for the business. In the afternoon, Marie fixed Winfred's lunch, put him in his
wheelchair, and pushed him out into the candy shop. "He took great
interest in what we were doing and could see things I couldn't see." It
also helped him pass the time. At night, Marie had an hour or so to sit
and talk with Winfred about the day, the shop, and the family. "He

would make observations about the work, our employees, and what needed to be done the next day."

The Kings continued to marvel at the success of the business, though time and time again they reminded themselves (as did others) that they were selling a "luxury item." Winfred and Marie would often remind each other, "If God is for us, who can be against us?"

◆   ◆   ◆

As she ran the candy business, Marie was evolving into an entrepreneur. She took pride in their product, and didn't apologize for what she sold. "Candy-makers are kind of conceited. But if you're not sold on your own product, what's the point of making it? They used to say I could sell icehouses to Eskimos. The power of persuasion is important. After awhile, I wasn't embarrassed to push my product, because I knew we had something good. I listened to public reaction (which was mostly good)…You have to listen to people's reactions, and be willing to change."

Like any business owner, Marie was always on the lookout for good workers. She spotted potential in Mary Yoder in the '60s, and again in Shirley Troyer in the early '70s. Mary remembers, "One day, out of the blue, Marie and Margaret came to call on me…After some small talk, Marie asked if I would be interested in working for her. What a question. Me? I didn't consider myself capable of doing such a thing. But she had a very convincing way and encouraged me to believe I could do it."

Following Winfred's sisters Margaret and Mabel, Winfred's sister-in-law Mary Lou, who was married to Herb, dipped for Marie in 1963. She also did some decorating, and even painted the kitchen, at Winfred's request. "Winfred was super to work for, and he was very particular about how things were to be done. I guess he liked my work, so he asked me to paint, and I didn't mind." Like Winfred and Herb, Marie and Mary Lou would grow close as well. "Marie was a very alive and energetic person. I know it was a trying time for her, and we could talk about anything. We shared a lot, and she was a good sister-in-law."

In addition to the family's challenges, Marie, Mary Lou, Winfred, and Herb saw the nation struggling as well, losing two significant leaders that same year—John F. Kennedy and Dr. Martin Luther King, Jr.

While she worked, Mary Lou noticed how well Winfred and Marie complemented each other. Winfred was effective at running and monitoring the business, as well as keeping the books. Marie executed all Winfred's plans. "To hear Marie describe it, Winfred was the 'head,' and she was the 'body.' It worked, and they were happy." She also noted how the two cared for each other—especially how Winfred protected Marie. "He didn't want anything done on Sunday. He didn't want to hear any pots banging or smell anything in the kitchen: 'No cooking!' he always said, not even for him. That was Marie's day off. He wanted her to go to church and go out to eat."

Keeping in line with family tradition, niece Sarah King, Everett's daughter, was also recruited by Marie. As a teenager, Sarah would print cards that labeled candy in the showroom, and she felt very special being responsible for that task. A few years later, Marie asked Sarah to work at the store, and she accepted. She waited on customers out front, and for Uncle Winfred she kept a detailed inventory of what each customer bought.

During Sarah's time at the store, Marie was a great influence, as she had been to so many others. Sarah says, "What I remember most was that she was the most attentive wife. She would get the candy cooking, and then she always had a period of time where she would go in and tend to Uncle Winfred's needs. She never complained and took wonderful care of him. At the time, when I was starting out my marriage and family, it really made an impression on me that I will never forget. She was so loving."

On one occasion, Marie attended a candy show in Columbus, Ohio, and asked Sarah to go along. "On the way, we had such a neat conversation. I kind of knew that Uncle Winfred had gotten sick when

I was younger, but now I was older. She went through the process of how he got sick, and how she started the business...the story of what they had gone through. I just remember thinking what a special lady this was, to do what she did, to take the role of provider. He had a large part in the decision-making, but she carried the workload. As the years rolled on, I will always remember how she was always positive, upbeat, and concerned about other people and about my family. I will never forget the impact that she had on people's lives by her example. She never made a big deal about what she did. It was her example that spoke volumes."

In the '70s, Marie's search for employees was motivated by her increasing physical limitations. Marie's arms were starting to give out after so many years of stirring, so she asked Shirley Troyer if she would be interested in working mornings at the candy store. Today, with such fond memories of Marie and her time there, Shirley is so glad she said yes. "She used to say to us girls as we were working, 'Now remember, if you can't work and talk at the same time, you know which one has to go!' We would smile, and we learned to do both quite well. She also used to encourage us to time ourselves to see how well we were working...This was a good teaching method, one I still use today."

Shirley was also impressed by the relationship that Marie and Winfred maintained as business partners and as husband and wife. "She was so dedicated to Winfred, and she would bring him out every afternoon in his wheelchair so he could sit out in the shop. We would visit with him and have a lot of laughs, but believe me, if he thought you were taking more steps to get something done than you needed, he would tell you. But I remember the good laughs. Marie would always say Winfred was sharp; he took care of the business part, and she 'couldn't do it without him.' But she did her part well too."

Mary tells of Winfred's keen sense of hearing. "Winfred used to call me from his bedroom, which was one wall away. 'Did you put both bags of brown sugar in that batch, Mary?' He knew the contents of each batch of candy. Winfred was very much a part of the business. He would come out in his wheelchair and often spend the afternoon with us ladies. He always had something interesting to share, having listened to the news, and we always looked forward to his visits." Ruth Lyon's *50/50 Club*, a television show well known for farm news and weather, was frequently enjoyed by Winfred at lunch.

Most of all, Shirley will remember Marie's "love and faithfulness she had for the Lord, the love for her family, the kindness she would show, and how I loved to hear her laugh—and we had a lot of those times!"

Mary remembers the same. "I personally do not remember ever hearing Marie complain about her assignment in life. She cared for Winfred willingly and gave up a lot of the normal activities of life. Her love and commitment to her God was what made her life so meaningful. She never hesitated to express her gratitude and love for her Savior Jesus Christ. She knows Him personally. He was her strength and comfort."

Along with God's grace and her willingness to take risks, Marie credits her and Winfred's trust in each other and ability to communicate well for the success of the business. It seemed that they were excellent partners. Winfred never allowed them to go to bed angry about anything, and his sense of humor helped as well. Over the course of their marriage, Winfred had pneumonia at least five times, so his lungs were very weak and he could not lie on his back all night. Because he couldn't turn himself from side to side, he would call Marie every two or three hours to get up and turn him. He saved up the jokes he read during the day and would share them with Marie when she came in. "He thought I wouldn't mind so much getting up if he could make me laugh."

"I don't think Winfred and I would have made it if we hadn't communicated as well as we did," Marie says. "It never entered my mind to leave him. In a marriage, you can't be selfish. Communication was what got us through...We'd talk all night sometimes. When I first went with him, that's what impressed me about him—he had something to say. We always had something to talk about. I think that's what brought us together, and that's what kept us together."

Winfred and Marie (brains and brawn) doing bookwork.

Winfred continued to keep the books, answer the telephone, and order supplies. He would also take care of 'giving orders' if Marie had to go away on business. He did much of the planning work for the business, day to day. Marie believes, "If I would have taken this away from him, he would not have lived as long as he did." Winfred was very good at this managerial side of the business, and Marie knew it was important for him to be a partner with her.

Winfred died in February of 1973. He had been in a hospital bed and wheelchair for more than thirty-two years. For those thirty-two years, he had been an inspiration to all who knew him or met him at the candy shop—but most of all, to his wife. "He did not complain to others. If ever I felt sorry for myself, he would say, 'There is no room for self-pity in this world,'" a philosophy reminiscent of Marie's father and the lessons she learned during her teenage years. "He had me buy a motto to hang by his bed that read 'Praise the Lord!' He said we just didn't praise the Lord enough, and he read his Bible much." Because of this attitude, Winfred was an inspiration to many. Friends, family, neighbors, and community members visited Winfred to encourage him—and they left being encouraged.

"The verse from Acts 3:8, 'Walking, leaping, and praising the Lord,' was the thing he wanted to do all his life—so now his dream and prayer had come true," Marie says.

After Winfred's death, Jay offered to help keep Marie's Candies running. "I realized without Winfred to push, to encourage, and to advise me, something had gone out of the business for me. It had gotten too big for me to do myself. I was happy that one of our children wanted to carry on the business that Winfred and I had started and worked so hard to build up with God's help."

Jay adding pecans to caramel squares to make Tur'kins (like Turtles).

Marie hand-dipping Tur'kins.

In May of 1977, Jay bought the business, and Marie moved into an apartment across town. Marie was ready to let him take over. Stirring candy and lifting Winfred for so many years had left her physically tired all the time, with sore shoulders to this day.

◆   ◆   ◆

As Jay and his wife, Kathy, took over Marie's Home Made Candies, it officially became a second-generation business. When they met in the early 1960s, while both were still in high school, they couldn't have predicted that making candy would become a partnership and their livelihood. But it seems there was much of the unpredictable for the King family.

At Salem High School, Jay was active in FFA and passionate about basketball. He played on two State tournament teams (1959 & 1960), and one State championship team (1960). When the boys played at Ohio State University for the state title, Jerry Lucas and a few other

OSU players showed the team around at St. John's Arena. With his mouth open, one of the boys, as if in a scene out of *Hoosiers*, said, "Wow. You could put a lot of hay in here." Both Marie and Kathy went to that state game, and when the players came home, they were met with a parade through Urbana. They were the town heroes.

High school would soon come to an end, though. Jay had never liked school and still wasn't sure what he wanted to do, so he worked construction for that first year after graduation. He rode his bike into town every morning and home every evening; after a few months, he had saved up enough money to buy a car, which Marie went with him to purchase. The following year, Jay decided to attend Goshen College in Indiana. He had enough money to attend for one year, and was motivated by the thought of playing basketball there. He didn't make the team, however, and spent the year taking general education classes. He still couldn't seem to find his niche. "I didn't apply myself, and it wasn't what I wanted to do at that point." He returned home to work construction again.

In 1963, Jay volunteered for a two-year term of service with 1-W, in lieu of the Armed Forces. It evolved into an opportunity to work as an X-ray orderly at Evanston Hospital near Chicago, Illinois. Kathy followed in the fall of 1964; she worked in surgery after having completed nurse's training at Mennonite Hospital School of Nursing, Bloomington, Illinois. After saving enough money for Kathy's engagement ring by working at a filling station from six to nine o'clock every night and on Saturdays and Sundays (while he worked at the hospital every day until five o'clock), Jay married Kathy on October 10, 1964.

Looking back, both Jay and Kathy are thankful for that experience—they had that year together, just the two of them. "We had no obligations; it was a good year of growing. We thought about staying there—we had good jobs, and it was a beautiful area—but we just felt that we wanted to come back," Jay says.

In September of 1965, Jay and Kathy returned home to West Liberty. Seth, their first son, was born in 1966; second son Shannon was born in August of 1968. Jay worked for Hostetler Construction until 1968, and then for Notestine Floor Covering until 1972, while Kathy was home with the boys. They both also helped out with the youth at church. However, after several years, "We got unsettled with the work we were doing." Winfred suggested Jay perhaps work half-days at the business, but Winfred wasn't sure that the business could support two families.

After much prayer and consideration, Jay and Kathy left in September of 1972 for Word of Life Institute in Schroon Lake, New York. There, they would go to school to become missionaries. They sold their house and their furniture; they were not planning on returning. "We weren't really planning on going into the business at that point," Jay says. The Kings thought they were headed for the mission field, and in fact, they were—though it wasn't the "field" they'd thought it would be.

Throughout that fall, their application for Unevangelized Field Missions lay untouched on their New York dining room table; they would never fill it out. For some reason, both Jay and Kathy were thinking about West Liberty.

They came home for Christmas in 1972. Jay helped his parents with odd jobs around the house, and he and Kathy both worked in the store. Of course, the holiday season was a busy time, and there was much to do. They returned to Schroon Lake in New York after Christmas—for the last time, though they didn't know it then.

Kathy remembers a Sunday evening after Winfred's funeral in 1973. Marie went to mix ingredients for the next day and said, "I just don't have the heart for this."

At the same time, both Jay and Kathy realized that from then on, Marie was going to need help. Winfred had been her best friend and the one she lived for; without him, Marie's motivation to run the business was gone. Jay recalls his father's death "definitely affecting the business because he was the one who ran it—the brains. He watched the finances and controlled that. He set the direction. Marie's motivation was him. He was able to guide her in how to get the work accomplished, how to do things, and how best to organize. I think it was a total loss to her. They had been so close for thirty-some years, day and night together. She was his lifeline. He couldn't do anything without her, and she couldn't do anything without him."

Neither Joe nor Dan was interested in helping with the business at this time, so Jay and Kathy knew it was up to them if the business would continue as a family endeavor. Joe was in Rushsylvania, Ohio, doing construction and masonry work, and Dan was in business in Cincinnati, Ohio, selling computers for Radio Corporation of America; he later owned a motel in the late '70s.

Brothers Joe, Jay, and Dan, Thanksgiving 1997.

Jay struggled with the decision for several years. Up to that point, he felt that the only worthy job was full-time Christian service. Even some Christian friends and acquaintances felt that Jay and Kathy were making a mistake. But Jay eventually came to a realization that helped him find peace in the decision he was about to make. "We're all in full-time Christian service," he says. "Wherever we are, we need to be totally serving Christ."

In the end, they never felt trapped by the situation unfolding. They knew it was where they were supposed to be, trusted that this was God's plan for them, and were thankful for His direction. It wasn't a *sacrifice* of their plans to go to the mission field or finish at Word of Life—it was just a *change* of plans. And a different "field."

◆   ◆   ◆

In spite of the transition the business went through after Winfred's death—Jay's taking over more responsibility, and Marie's "phasing out"—the business did go right on.

"Mom was really good," Jay remembers. "She was determined that she wasn't going to sit and sulk. She said at different times, 'I'm just not going to sit and feel sorry for myself.' Right away, she got involved, visited people, and took a trip." Though she was cutting back the hours she put in at the store, she was not slowing down—that wasn't Marie's style. She had always been a woman on the go, with people to serve and a family to take care of. Marie's niece Joan Zook remembers loving to ride with Marie during the government-enforced thirty-five-mile-per-hour speed limits (as a gasoline conservation measure) of World War II, because Marie liked to exceed the speed limit. She always said to Joan, "I don't have time to go just thirty-five."

Helping people was a "job" from which Marie would never retire. As her work decreased at the store, she gave her time to others in a different fashion. She and sister Geneva answered an advertisement in the local paper looking for volunteers to answer phones for a crisis hotline out of Urbana, Ohio, to serve the citizens of Logan, Champaign, and Clark counties. They went to twelve hours of training, took calls two nights per week, and attended a monthly meeting. Marie would con-

tinue this work for eighteen years, and served on the hotline's adminis-
trative board for six years.

Still, Jay continued to learn from Marie when she was at the store.
"She taught me. She told me how to do things, she taught me how to
mix different batches of candy, but she did step back and let me go
right ahead. Even to this day, we still use her recipes. We don't change
them unless there's some drastic need to do so. Sometimes, when she
wasn't there, I would often have to go to the staff who had worked for
her, and were now working for me, and ask, 'Now how do you do this?
Or 'How does this work?'"

Of all the employees, Margaret was probably the most helpful
regarding Jay's acclimation to the business. She was a steady, consistent
packer, and had such a long history working for the candy shop that
she was known for her customer service. Often times, customers would
mistake her for Marie. In early years, she would correct them, but as
time went on, she didn't. (With a grin, Kathy suggests the Margaret
liked the attention). She was incredibly reliable and devoted to the
business; in fact, Jay couldn't even convince her to take a day off. Margaret had a schedule, and days off were not part of it. "What would I
do?" she would always say to Jay. It seemed she considered the store a
kind of partner, and took her work very seriously. When friends and
relatives would tease her about marrying or meeting a nice man, she
would again respond with a question: "Why would I need one of
those?"

Marie would continue to participate in the business for another four
or five years after Winfred's death, but she didn't tie herself down to it.
She would hand-dip or wrap, take phone orders, or wait on customers
out front. And as Jay and Kathy learned the business, she would often
watch their daughter Rebecca, who was born in 1976.

Jay regrets not being able to work with his dad in the business for a
while, and knows he would have learned from Winfred's wisdom and
experience had they worked side by side. "When I was younger, I used
to tell Dad, 'You don't have to work that hard.' He and Mom would

kind of just smile. I didn't know what I was talking about. I was naive. I had no idea what running this business took."

◆　　　◆　　　◆

Throughout the 1980s, as Marie's Candies ("Home Made" was dropped from the official name in the '70s) continued to thrive, Jay and Kathy opened two other stores. The Springfield Market Place store ran from 1980 through the Christmas of 1986, and their Bellefontaine store opened just before Thanksgiving in 1984. That store didn't close until 1997. Not only did Jay and Kathy run a business—they also raised a family. Seth, Shannon, and Rebecca all helped out with operations at the store, and living in a house attached to a candy shop was routine for them, just as it was for Jay during his childhood.

Marie's granddaughter and Jay and Kathy's daughter, Rebecca, making her daily rounds in the shop, 1979.

Like Jay when he was young, both Seth and Shannon would help with candy making and cleaning. Seth recalls, "In the mornings, we'd get up and help Dad with the Peppermint Chews—starting in the sixth grade, all the way through high school. I remember waking up and hearing him pull the Chews...That meant it was time to get up there and help him. We mopped the floors every Saturday on our hands and knees." Shannon remembers Seth getting the "easiest parts to mop...even after football games on Friday nights. Shannon and I would split up the yard mowing in the summer, and we also did odd jobs like painting the storage shed or putting up Christmas lights on the trees in front of the shop."

Rebecca says, "I would help stack the chocolate bunnies when I was little. In high school, I would work, and I hated it at holidays, because my friends were always relaxing and I had to work. I wasn't grateful for the job. I just wanted to be able to take it easy for selfish reasons. In college, I felt like I was a gofer. I wasn't at all grateful for the business. I think in any family business, you have to go away to appreciate what it did for you."

All three children graduated from West-Liberty Salem High School, Seth and Shannon both having successful football careers and going on to play at Wheaton College and Taylor University respectively, and Rebecca having successful volleyball and track seasons, going on to play and run at Taylor.

Now a part of the business, Shannon reflects, "I guess certain things were expected when we were in high school, but...we didn't work a ton because we were always playing sports...We didn't work as much as we should have."

All three kids are equally thankful and impressed that Jay and Kathy were always at their games, matches, and races, in spite of the work the store demanded. "I'm sure they didn't miss anything in high school. I'm positive. I'm sure Dad didn't miss a football game in college. I don't know how they did it—I'm sure they had things to do and were tired," Shannon says.

While the boys and Rebecca were away at school, Jay and Kathy began to enjoy some time to themselves—when they weren't traveling to watch games, or taking care of the two other stores. Always enjoying each other's company, they made time for vacations, reading together, and bicycling, especially when the weather was nice in West Liberty.

◆　　　◆　　　◆

What is now affectionately referred to by the Kings as "the depot project" started with those family bike rides. In the evenings and on the weekends in the early '90s, the Kings would admire an abandoned train depot on the outskirts of town. Interested in history and West Liberty's heritage, Jay and Kathy would often discuss the depot on their walks or rides. Jay says, "We would even walk right up to it. We would say, 'It's really too bad that this thing's going to pieces. Somebody ought to do something with it.'" They learned that the depot had been built in 1926, thirty years before the official birth of Marie's Candies. In 1930, New York Central Railroad took over the day-to-day operations of both freight and passengers and ran it into the 1940s. The last passenger was Bill King, on his way home from WWII in 1942. Freight continued to be received at the depot until 1960.

The Kings had heard different speculation regarding what the city might do with the depot; apparently, blueprints had been drawn for its move further into town, by the railroad tracks, and conversion into a library. Another idea was that the Lions Club would relocate the depot to the park.

Jay and Kathy began dreaming. What if they bought the depot and converted it into a new showroom for their candies? The business was doing well, and they could use the extra space. "We ended up going to Alvin King, who owned the feed mill where the depot sat," Jay says. Despite its crumbling façade, apparently the depot was being used as a grain bin. "There was a pipe in the roof that they would use to pipe grain in, but we had heard they were going to tear it down or move it out of town."

King, though indeed interested in having space for more modern grain elevators, said he needed to talk to the village, because he had essentially given the depot to them. Shortly after, West Liberty officials agreed that the Kings could attempt to buy the depot, and Alvin said he was willing to sell.

In order for the candy shop to expand and add the depot, the Kings would need additional land. At this time, Bob Godwin owned the rental property beside Marie's—the space they would need for the expansion. Jay recalls, "Before we bought the depot, we approached Bob. He agreed to sell the rental property. Evidently, God was working ahead of us, because I really didn't think he would sell it."

The Kings contacted Merkle Heavy Moving, from Ohio City, and Joe Kauffman, a local contractor, about doing the work for them. They asked Kauffman to put a new roof on the depot, and Merkle, after coming down to look at the property, said that he and his crew could move the depot. The Kings thought they had a buyer for the house on the rental property, but as they went further along, those plans crumbled. Nothing seemed to be working out, and nobody seemed to want the house. It was going to cost them a considerable amount of money to have the house torn down. It was hardly something that Jay and Kathy wanted to pay for, as inside, "The house was really bad. It was just a mess." They didn't know what would be better—pay to have the house torn down, or pay to have it moved and restored.

As they made decisions about where to go next with the project, the Kings contacted Steve Gray in San Francisco, California, an expert in historic preservation whose parents lived in West Liberty, for advice. Steve, a graduate of the University of Florida's architecture program, had made the first wooden sign for the business in 1978, and Jay and Kathy had been happy with his work. They sent him several pictures of the depot so, alongside them, he could begin developing a vision for the project.

After Gray saw the pictures of the run-down building, he knew that the first year's effort would simply involve moving and then stabilizing the heavily deteriorated depot structurally. But he also knew the Kings wanted direction regarding the depot, how to make it part of the business, and what to do with the rental house and property. Ultimately, Gray's vision was to unify all the buildings (the current candy shop the Kings were operating out of, the depot, and the rental house), either by physically connecting the structures, or by unifying them with color, design, signage, lighting, and/or landscaping.

At Jay and Kathy's request, Gray considered the rental house specifically. "My background is in preservation. Even though it was a benign little tract house, I still couldn't see destroying a building. I just kind of said off the cuff, 'Why don't you consider saving it?' and Jay took me very seriously, which I'm glad about now. It was a significant financial investment to add that to the project, but now well worth it." Jay remembers Steve saying, "We'll put the same color on it, and it will be like a complex here."

At Gray's encouragement, the Kings contacted the mover again and asked him if he could move the house; he said he could. The house would eventually end up behind the depot, fully restored, and Jay had discovered a potential purpose for it: "We thought we could use it for our missionary friends from Indonesia. We wanted them to be able to live in it."

By the summer of 1993, they were nearly ready to move the actual depot itself, but Joe King (Jay's brother) and "Digger Dan" Yoder first had to do excavation work at the new site and put in a basement.

When that work was completed, Jay and Kathy soon learned just how complex moving an entire building from one end of town to the other could be. They worked with Dayton Power & Light Co, the phone company, and the cable companies to ensure a smooth move. The entire move took much preparation, but Lester Merkle was confident about his crew's ability to move the fragile house and depot unharmed. He said, "When I move a house, you can leave a glass of water sitting on the table and I won't spill it."

Jay was a part of the moving preparations as well. "I had to go through town with tree trimmers and ask if we could trim trees so the depot could come through. We really had to work on a route. The best route had high wattage power wires, so we had to choose a different route. At one point, we had to go over a bridge that had railings that were too narrow. The depot had to be lifted up above these railings."

In all, the three-mile move took about five hours. They started at nine o'clock in the morning, and it was twelve-thirty or one o'clock when the depot finally arrived at its destination. Kathy recalls, "It was a huge parade that day. They sold all the film at the drugstore and the IGA."

After the depot had been moved, Gray made one of only two trips he would make to West Liberty during the entire depot project. Amazingly, the Kings and Gray did all of their work—designing and decision-making—by phone, fax machine, and e-mail. Gray recalls, "Jay and Kathy defined their basic store needs and functions. They were thinking of rebuilding the inside more than we ended up doing, but I felt strongly that we could maintain the original inside of the depot. They were so open to my suggestions, very trusting, and really listened to my input. Overall, design and planning took about a year. There was a lot going on; really we were talking about the whole identity of Marie's—-color scheme, logo, packaging, and boxes—one big sweep of change. I feel really strongly that everything should be coordinated. They completely trusted me with that, and the teal blue became a strong theme for everything."

After two years of outside work and renovation, the Kings made it their goal to open the depot in 1996—the fortieth anniversary of the business. Electricians, plumbers, and heating/cooling technicians all had to be hired to implement and execute Gray's vision for the inside restoration. Jay and Kathy knew their work was far from over; it took about four to six months to complete the inside of the depot. But even today, it's hard to miss the enthusiasm in Jay's voice as he recalls the project. "We tried to keep it as much like it was originally as we could. Steve had great ideas to maintain the original element of the depot, and we did research about what the original lights and other fixtures would have looked like. Eventually, we had to hire a local architect, Don Lee from Bellefontaine, Ohio, to draw up plans that would be state approved."

Gray, like others who work with and for the Kings, was blessed by the family during the project. He discovered "the joy of working with a client who was putting the future of what the business was going to look like in my hands. They never argued with a single thing, and they gave me so much freedom to do what I needed. It was significant because a lot of people were watching. They let criticism roll away and kept looking ahead. And they always sent me away with a lot of candy," Gray says, laughing.

The admiration was mutual. Kathy reminisces, "It would get pretty tense and pretty stressful sometimes; it was just constant. We couldn't quit making candy while all the decisions were being made. We'd have to call Steve and often have him directly talk to the contractors and the electricians. Through it all, he was just amazing."

She also remembers the project being more work than they had anticipated. "We'd say to each other and laugh, 'Whose idea was this?' But we never got to the point that we fumed and fussed and would fight about it. The closest I got to feeling really bad was the day of the open house, and not being ready with all those people coming Friday night."

Depot ribbon cutting (provided by The Ambassadors), Thanksgiving
Open House, 1996.

"Friday night" was the invitation-only open house the Kings held
on Thanksgiving weekend in 1996. Five hundred invitations went out
to contractors, movers, and so many others who had helped with the
project. Gray traveled to Ohio several days prior from San Francisco to
help with finishing details. That day, the glass showcase was being
installed and all the candy needed to be transferred. The stained glass
window, created by Vera Sickles, depicting Marie and her life, was
completed at roughly five o'clock that afternoon. Though it was stressful, the evening was both a success and a celebration. There were no
sales that evening: "We had candy sitting everywhere. The guests could
eat all the candy they wanted," Kathy says.

Depot architect, Steve Gray, and Marie at the Depot Open House.

The next day was an open house for the community. "We weren't ready, but we did it," Kathy says with a smile. In the end, the project was an incredible success. The building, both inside and out, was beautiful. With much of the original lighting and woodwork, pictures of the old train station, railroad memorabilia and signs (purchased at auctions and from antique collectors Gomer Poole and Pee Wee Arbogast), and a breathtaking fifteen-foot stained glass portrait of Marie, the depot succeeded in honoring both the town of West Liberty and the humble woman who helped put it on the map.

Stained glass window.

In September 2000, the depot showroom and the actual candy shop (where the candy is made, packed, and stored) were connected. Jay and Steve knew that those buildings wouldn't be connected initially, but still drew up plans that would allow for the connection eventually.

This work, done by Jeff Heiberger and Larry Pearson, was a "necessary convenience," as the Kings and employees were carrying candy downstairs and outside between the two buildings, covering the candy in foul weather. The connector room now displays old candy advertisements and paraphernalia, Kathy's collections of chocolate pots, Marie's Fiesta Ware, and thirty chairs and a slide projector. When tours come through, Kathy speaks, three to four times a month, on the history of chocolate, candy making, and the advent of Marie's.

"Overall, we thought it was going to be a simple thing, and it turned into a monstrous project. The move alone took so much coordination. There was always a mess. We probably both got a little older through the whole thing," both Jay and Kathy laugh.

The finished "Depot Project."

◆　　　◆　　　◆

While growing up literally in a candy shop, the three heirs-apparent learned more than just what Peppermint Chews ought to look like or how many Peanut Butter Fancies went into a one-pound assortment.

This was no ordinary business, and this was no ordinary family. Their heritage as Kings was a privilege, and the lessons they learned about how to behave and how to treat people were far more important than what they learned about the business of candy making. And that makes sense. Because really, Marie's was, and continues to be, about so much more than candy. It's about caring for people, partnering with neighbors, doing the right thing, and striving to be a blessing to others. These were the lessons that would endure.

Of Marie, the grandchildren have fond memories. The boys remember staying with Marie, or taking trips to the five and dime or the zoo with her; Rebecca reminisces about bike rides, picnics, and tea parties. Of course, all three grandchildren loved spending time with Marie when they were young, whether it was working with her or playing. Seth was impressed by her emotional strength over the years. "I have never seen Grandma upset or in a bad mood. The only time I ever saw her get teary-eyed was when she would talk about Grandpa King. I never saw her mad or angry. I know her faith is very important, and I think she lived that out. She was also a hard worker, and I'm sure that's where my dad got a lot of his drive and example."

Shannon's memories are similar. "I remember doing hard candy with Grandma. She did most of it, but I helped and she told 'Ready Freddie' stories. They were really about me, but she said they were about a boy named Freddie who was always ready to work or play. Sometimes I remember saying 'Grandma, I've already heard that one.'"

Shannon learned life lessons from Marie, too. "She was an incredibly hard worker; she even laid an outdoor brick fireplace at one point. She can't lift her arms because of all she did." Apart from the physical, he says, "Grandma is always quoting scripture. She's always talking about doing what's right and being kind. She doesn't have one bad thing to say about anyone." Shannon also credits lessons in determination to Marie. "Grandma never gave up. I mean she *never* gave up. She just kept going. No matter how bad it gets, you just keep going."

Rebecca's interaction with Marie was different from her brothers', because Marie had retired by the time Rebecca was old enough to remember learning specific lessons from her. "She was always very content and happy in life. She did things for others and gave of her time to help others. When I would stay with her, she would answer the phone and just listen to people. She would give of her time at church. She was an elder/deacon, a greeter. When she had her car and was able to drive, she would always go visit people in the hospital or at home—not just old and sick, but young mothers. She taught me to be giving and to care about other people."

They learned just as many lessons from their parents as well, especially about how to run a business or work with people in general.

"Never once have I ever heard him [Jay] swear. I have a lot of respect for him for that. And just the way he works…I've never seen any other man work as hard as my dad does. That's definitely one thing that stands out about my dad," says Seth. "And I remember Mom being home a lot, too. I don't ever remember her being gone. She was always there."

"They also taught me to always remember who you are, and what you are, and that it's never wrong to do right, and never right to do wrong," Seth continues. "Dad always went out of his way—his philosophy was that the customer was always right. He never let his frustration show. He takes care of his employees, and they are loyal because of that. He's a very demanding employer…but he has a soft spot for people. From him, I learned as a supervisor to take care of your people. You always do things right, even if it means extra effort or money. You don't cut corners."

Shannon says his parents taught him morals and values. "Dad always says 'We always need to do what's right; we always need to do the right thing no matter what.' They taught us to always treat others with respect, and to bend over backwards for people—that has been modeled more than that's been said. Mom and Dad never said one bad thing about people. All through college and high school, I never remember them having one bad thing to say about anyone. You always get up after you've been knocked down....Dad, every morning, no matter what, always spends time in the Word, and I've learned that."

Jay and Kathy's influence on Rebecca has been no different. "Hard work is probably the biggest thing they've taught me. You do your best, regardless of the results...You work as hard as you can, because that's what God would want you to do. Live for God...Live your life the right way and do the right thing. Being considerate of others was always important at our house too, and not saying a bad word about anyone."

◆　　　◆　　　◆

Steve Strickland, who has worked at Marie's since 1987, is pulling Peppermint Chews this morning. He admits that when he first started sixteen years ago, it took him a couple weeks to feel comfortable pulling. Now, he does it with precision and skill. Starting each morning around 7:45, he usually isn't done until roughly 9:30—when he has pulled the second of two slabs of Peppermint Chews from the mix that Jay measured out the night before (Jay and Shannon have long finished pulling and cutting the first batch).

He seems a bit nervous that someone is watching; not nervous about what he's doing, but perplexed as to what an observer could possibly be writing about the process. The candy material is very dark, almost black, with the look and texture of an eel; but it smells of peppermint, of course, and Steve is kneading it on a marble island that is lightly covered with grease. After he works with the material, he's ready to sling it on the original hook Marie used. He slings and twists, back and forth, almost rhythmically with the '50s music in the background, the candy that is now light in color, blonde like Rapunzel's hair, until it "feels" right. When the candy starts to split or thin out into strings, he knows it's time to move on to the next step. He then takes it over to a metal countertop behind a plastic curtain (to protect the rest of the room from a settling layer of powdered sugar), twists it out, and cuts it into half-inch rectangles on the original cutter that Marie used. Another employee helps cover the candy in powdered sugar, and after that it will go to the enrober (French for "to cover"), where it will be slathered in chocolate. Four days a week, thirty pounds each time is Steve's routine, to make the delicacy for which Marie has become famous, the delicacy of which customers never tire. Even Winfred ate one dark chocolate, one milk chocolate, and one white chocolate Peppermint Chew, together, every night.

Marie's operates with two enrobers, one with a ten-inch belt for dark production (purchased in 1982—all candy prior to that was hand-dipped), and one with a sixteen-inch belt for milk production (purchased in 1998). Both sit in the long room that used to be the sales area. Household items are used in creative ways for candy production, such as hair dryers (to melt chocolate that sticks to sides of the chocolate pot), hand-held mirrors to check to backsides of pieces of candy, and a hammer to break ten-pound slabs of chocolate. As the candy comes through the enrober, an employee stands by the belt to "string" the candy by hand—giving it a mark to identify its type.

Journalist Miriam Baeir notes, "Tranquility and order rule at Marie's, but candy eating is encouraged. The employees may eat their fill of any of the treats, and leading the way may be Mr. King himself. 'I eat it all day long,' Jay laughed, adding there was a time when he ate at least a pound of candy a day."[9]

The kitchen behind the old sales area is still the candy kitchen. One step south is the room that has served as the office since the house was built in 1966. The home kitchen, the bedrooms, and the living room all serve as storage areas now, either for candy or for gift items. Shannon's "office" is in a small cubby—literally, with a clip light and an old adding machine for office furniture—in one of the storage rooms.

Downstairs, the old family room is now an area for wrapping and sending out mail orders. There is also a packing area where four ladies sit taking candy from brown cardboard boxes (where it goes after it cools off the enrober) and placing them in boxes for sale. A new cold room for the candy storage was recently added as an attempt to be better prepared for the Christmas season.

Rebecca working on www.mariescandies.com.

Presentation has become just as much a part of the business as production. Both Kathy and Rebecca understand the importance of an attractive showroom; they want the depot to be inviting. Both have attended a special merchandising school for candy-makers/sellers. Apparently, there is a technique to presenting and even *lighting* candy. At the spring 2003 Malley School of Merchandising in Cleveland, Ohio, Mary Beth Gotti taught candy-makers about "light and color and its effects on your chocolates." (It would seem this *is* serious business; Gotti played a key role in the re-lamping of New York's Statue of Liberty). In addition, Jay and Kathy joined Retail Confectioner's International (RCI) in 1978, which they have found to be "truly helpful," according to Kathy. The organization, founded in 1918, is composed of approximately 150 independently owned candy businesses in both the states and abroad. They sponsor three to four conventions annually in different cities in the U.S. that include speakers, clinics, and how-to seminars. Jay supports these endeavors to make the candy shop as successful as it can be. He settles for nothing less than excellence, and with more than thirty years in the business, he says, "You never quit learning."

Jay's Retail Confectioner's International Board picture, taken in Chicago, June 2002.

Their personal service also draws much attention and even more business. The Kings make candy for customers with special dietary needs (Kathy herself is diabetic). In the past, they have made mints to match swatches of bridal fabric. There have even been diamond engagement rings and diamond earrings placed in boxes of candy over the years.

Mary Lou King says, "Marie is so proud of Jay and Kathy. They've done such a wonderful job with the business; I know the family is proud of them. And I know Winfred would love what they've done. I can't say enough about them."

Jay and wife, Kathy, in June 2002.

Marie's Candies continues to thrive—in part because of their quality product, and in part because of their emphasis on customer service. It seems that people can't get enough of either. In December 1946, before the "business" was a full-time enterprise, Marie sold nearly twelve hundred pounds of candy. During the Christmas season of 2002, Marie's Candies sold approximately twenty-four thousand pounds of candy. For Easter 1947, Marie sold more than one hundred cream-filled eggs. For Easter 2003, Marie's sold more than eighty-five hundred. A family business that started with a woman and a man and the help of their three sons has evolved into a shop that now employs thirty people throughout the year (eleven full-time).

Future

The past returning through another gate.

—Arnold H. Glasgow

Marie, Jay, Kathy, Seth, Shannon, and Rebecca all have dreams about where Marie's will go in this new century. Some of those dreams are the same, while some are vastly different. All of them will testify to the unexpected blessing the candy shop has been, and consider it to be so much more than a professional enterprise. Marie's Candies *is* their family, and the future holds promise—and certainly more of the unexpected.

Marie says, "It's wonderful that it's a family project. That's the only way it will survive. None of us trained for this; we just learned the hard way, using wisdom, common sense, and experimentation to learn...That seems to work. I hope Seth wants to be there, too, but I'm not sure. I think he might be there in the end. We'll see what happens. I don't push them. They have to be willing to come of their own free will. That's how it was with Jay."

Jay has all along been motivated by work itself and the intangible rewards of the business ("I don't do it for the money. That's not why I do it"). "My dad always thought that he would like to be able to totally support a missionary. We enjoy supporting several missionaries in smaller amounts. It's exciting to be able to meet others' needs when they arise."

Kathy speaks to his drive. "He's definitely work-oriented. His whole family [considers] work a virtue."

Jay admits, "I've always enjoyed working hard. Work *is* a virtue. It's fun to produce a good product. We work hard at giving service. And if something goes wrong, we always look for an opportunity to make it right. We work at that and we feel an accomplishment with that. And we're here now. This business is ours now—we bought it in 1977. We moved that depot and restored it. That's kind of a motivator, to see that accomplished. I enjoy the results of making candy and seeing people enjoy it. I enjoy providing a job for people....Starting a business, building a business, buying the depot—those have been exciting, motivational things. That's been an encouraging thing to see that. Maintaining a business is hard, and that's where we are now."

Both Jay and Kathy explain that there are very few third-generation candy businesses, but they are realistic about the future and the role their children may or may not play in the business. "If they sold it, I would understand. It's not something that I feel has to happen. It was probably more important for my parents to see it go on than for me." However, he admits, "It would be nice to see the business go on. It would even be exciting to see all three of our children involved. Whether that ever happens, I don't know. Whether it would be the best thing, I don't know. Candy-maker friends of ours say 'only one child' in the business. But, I would like to pass it on. It's always been kind of a dream that it would be neat to have family who would take it over. There are a lot of possibilities; the business could grow by leaps and bounds if they wanted to move that direction."

In August 1998, Shannon resigned his position at the Ohio State Highway Patrol to join the business. It has been a good move for him, allowing for more time with his family at work and his family at home. Rebecca joined in November 2001, and has relieved Kathy's workload incredibly. Currently, Rebecca assists Kathy and takes care of all on-line orders and web site maintenance. Seth works for the Urbana Police Department, but hasn't completely ruled out working with the business eventually. The three all have a vision of the future for Marie's Candies.

Shannon sees daily how much work and organization it takes to run the business. "There's a ton of stuff you could do; even streamline things on the computer. If Seth came in, we'd want to expand and add more equipment. Right now, there are all these main areas: sales, shipping, on-line, packaging, paperwork, production, inventory." All those areas require a major focus and a number of man-hours. "I've cut back maybe a little for Dad, but I don't do as much as probably could be done. Dad just does so much. It's really incredible. If Seth came in, it would really help a lot. Somebody probably really needs to take over overseeing production (other than Dad). I don't do a lot of that, and that would really help Dad."

Shannon pauses and says with a smirk, "If Rebecca wasn't so lazy, she could do that too. You can put that in there [the book]." It seems the grandchildren have inherited Marie's sense of humor. Rebecca chuckles, while Shannon continues.

Shannon

"My biggest job here is making sure we have what we need," he says. "Some days what takes up a lot of time is shrink-wrapping the final product, but…shrink-wrapping doesn't take any pressure off of Dad. I do a lot of stocking and moving boxes around all day. I make a little bit of candy, but not much." He finishes a batch of Peppermint Chews every morning and he occasionally helps with making mints or stirring creams.

Shannon believes that the business, in order to succeed in the future, will require a focus that it doesn't presently have. "What I'd like to see is...one piece of candy that's a signature."

At the same time, expansion is appealing. Jay and Kathy know they have a quality product. Shannon continues, "I know we could do well in a larger city, and sure, you'd like to see that."

Rebecca has enjoyed being around her older brother at work and knows that what he contributes helps Jay and Kathy immensely. "I think it's great; when he came back, he really helped Mom and Dad. I love having him around and hope he'll continue to be involved."

She also agrees with Shannon regarding making decisions about what's most important to them; she too seems torn between scaling back and expanding. "We both feel the frustration of going so many directions with the hundreds of products that we offer...but if we get bigger, we'll have to let go of a lot of the control."

From a distance, Seth is glad to see his younger brother and sister involved in the family business, and definitely sees the benefits of such involvement. Seth has fond memories of growing up in that environment, and wouldn't mind his own kids having the experience as well. He too sees the potential for growth, but knows that will have to be developed by someone other than his parents. "I like the idea of it being a unique store...that the only place you can get Marie's candies is in West Liberty, Ohio. But I also see the possibilities of expanding the business and moving into larger metropolitan areas. The product is second to none...and I think it would sell there. But, that's going to require a lot of capital to expand, and I don't think my dad has the energy to take that on himself."

Regarding Jay and Kathy, Seth seemed most willing to voice what all three kids think. "My dad works way too hard—my parents need to take it easy and travel." They are all grateful for the life their parents provided them—now they'd like to see Jay and Kathy enjoy this time of their lives.

Jay and Kathy with family at Bald Head Island, North Carolina. Top from left to right: Shannon, Jake, Joanie, Claire, Seth. Middle: Mya, Chloe, Michael. Bottom: Amber, Carson, Jay, Kathy, Rebecca.

Epilogue

"I will utter hidden things, things from of old—what we have heard and known, what our fathers have told us. We will not hide them from their children; we will tell the next generation the praiseworthy deeds of the Lord, his power, and the wonders he has done...so the next generation would know them, even the children yet to be born, and they in turn would tell their children. Then they would put their trust in God and would not forget his deeds but would keep his commands."

—Psalm 78: 2-4, 6-7

In the 1990s, Marie began her speaking tour and continued to be both enthusiastic about and involved in the candy-making business, informally and jokingly calling herself their "PR person." Marie has often told her story to audiences—more than one hundred times, in fact. At first, these public speaking engagements made her nervous. Then, to settle herself down and clear the air, she told herself that the people in the audience "put their pantyhose on one leg at a time, just like I do." That trick seemed to calm her nerves and put her at ease. The five pounds of Butter Creams she brought with her seemed to put the audience at ease as well.

By now, Marie has retired from her public speaking career, as it is much harder for her to get around. However, she was and is always eager to share her and Winfred's story—reminding each listener that it is God's story. "Everyone has a story to tell. Just not everyone has the words or writes it down." What does she want people to know about her story?

"I pray about that. I don't want to leave the wrong impression. I'm not trying to brag about anything. I couldn't have done any of this, anything without God's help. I want people to see that they are important in God's eyes and in this world. That they can make the most of what God has given them, even if that doesn't seem like much. I didn't have much, but God still used me. God expects you to do what you can right where you are. Bloom where you are."

She says, "In case you are thinking, 'My, she sure did have it all together. She made it sound so easy,' I want to tell you, it wasn't easy. I didn't always pray and wait for the answers. I'm an impatient person, one who likes things to happen right now! I didn't always cope with things too well, and I made a lot of mistakes. But God forgave me, and that's the only reason I am where I am today. Complete weakness and dependence on God will always be the occasion for the Spirit of God to manifest His power.

"We give God the credit for our candy business succeeding as it has. There were many disappointments and discouragements, but our faith in the Lord has been the thing that has sustained us, guarded us, and helped us to prosper. Years ago, I asked the Lord to give me a smile so I could bring glory to His name, and He gave me a smile. Proverbs 16:20 says 'God blesses those who obey him; happy is the man who puts his trust in the Lord.'"

◆   ◆   ◆

"Holy, fair, and wise is she;
The heaven such grace did lend her,
That she might admired be…"
　　　　　—Shakespeare's *The Two Gentlemen of Verona* (IV, ii, 45)

Notes

1. P. xvii. Clark, Thomas Curtis and Esther Gillespie. *Quotable Poems: An anthology of Modern Verse.* Willett, Clark, & Colby: New York. 1928. 128.

2. P. 26. *This Fabulous Century: 1940-1950.* Time Life Books: New York. 1969.

3. P. 28. Hill, Richard. "A Being Breathing Thoughtful Breath: The History of the British Iron Lung, 1832-1995." *History of the British Iron Lung.* 7 August 2003.
http://www.geocities.com/ironlungmuseum/ironlung.htm.

4. P. 30. "A Brief History of Polio." *Polio Information Center Online (PICO) History.* 19 November 2002. 6 August 2003.
<cumicro2.cpmc.columbia.edu/PICO/Chapters/History.html>

5. P. 30. "Polio and the Era of Fear." *The Mission.* University of Texas Health and Science Center at San Antonio. 6 August 2003.
www.uthscsa.edu/mission/fall94/polio.htm.

6. P. 31. This Fabulous Century.

7. P. 34. This Fabulous Century.

8. P. 40. Koch, Roy S. "Out of Adversity, Light." *Christian Living.* February 1968: 12-13.

9. P. 80. Baeir Miriam. "Kings of Candyland." *The Bellefontaine Examiner.* 13 February 1999.

0-595-29360-3